PEARLS

PEARLS

THE COMPLETE
MR & MRS PHILPOTT POEMS

Helena Nelson

HappenStance Press

ISBN: 978-1-9910131-67-1

Acknowledgements:

The author is grateful to editors who first published some of these poems:
Gerry Cambridge in *The Dark Horse*; Michael Mackmin in *The Rialto* (and
in *Starlight on Water,* 2003); and James Robertson of Kettillonia Press. Two
poems also appeared previously in *Plot and Counter-Plot* (Shoestring, 2010),
for which thanks to John Lucas. Thanks to Michael Mackmin for suggesting
the dowitcher in the poem 'Bird-Watcher'. Thanks to Jamie Rose for Mrs P's
hair. Thanks to Marcia Menter for insight and pearls.

By the same author:

POETRY

Branded (Red Squirrel Press, 2019)

Down With Poetry! (Happen*Stance*, 2016)

Plot and Counter-Plot (Shoestring Press, 2010)

Unsuitable Poems (Happen*Stance*, 2005)

Starlight on Water (Rialto, 2003)

Mr & Mrs Philpott on Holiday at Auchterawe (Kettillonia, 2002)

PROSE

How (Not) to Get Your Poetry Published (Happen*Stance*, 2016)

NOTE FOR VISUALLY IMPAIRED READERS:

The front jacket is a painting of Mr and Mrs Philpott asleep in bed. They
lie facing each other, eyes shut. Mr P is slightly higher on the pillows,
protective in position. Mrs P's head rests against his shoulder. She has long
silver hair in a braid that falls over a quilt patterned with stars, squares
and birds. He is mostly bald and his forehead is worry-lined. Behind the
headboard is a window, with curtains looped open. The main colours are
mauve, blue, white and silver. A mauve band halfway down the quilt holds
the book title (silver), then subtitle and author's name centred in very
dark blue. The back jacket is mauve with no images, just descriptive blurb,
followed by the complete text of 'Communication' (from page 107).

First published in 2022 by Happen*Stance* Press
https://happenstancepress.com

Printed and bound by Imprint Digital, Exeter
https://digital.imprint.co.uk

CONTENTS

There is a story

and what happens as it turns and turns and turns again
towards the end, the absolute end—because there has
to be one, doesn't there? There must be a proper *end*
though the thought of it could drive you round
the bend. And that's the thing—it is a bend
followed by still another and another
and another, each pretending to be
The Very End, thus contributing
confusion, given that the end
is an illusion and never
the end, which always
lurks around a
future bend
that isn't
here
yet

— | —

Widowed

Christmas is a bad time to die. Bad.
It wasn't as if she was old. Thin—
yes—but she'd always been thin, she didn't
approve of food. Unforgiving
and graceful and thin. Good with children,
fond of dogs, but distant to him.
Too much between them had gone unsaid.

She would have been fifty-five in May. May
or might—this time he was on his own.
She felt a pain, they did some kind of scan
and kept her in. She greyed to stone
in a week—and was gone. Neither son
could believe it. They paced. They frowned.
He should have *known*, they said. What could he say?

He didn't know what to say, had never known.
If he brought flowers, she would ask why.
She had never let him see her cry.
She had never let him see. In some agony
of her own, she didn't let him in. He wouldn't pry.
They weren't the sort of people who are happy.
At her request, after the ceremony
she was scattered as ash. Winnowed and blown.

So much between them had come untied.
Bride. Wife. Thirty years married,
unfastened, undone. In his head
he thought he was mad. He should have made
more of her, made more of love. But the funeral bed
was too full of ashes. If she'd just *said*—
if he had been less afraid—less terrified—
but she was gone. After she died, he prayed.

After

At the kitchen window
in his dressing-gown
he stands alone.
His sons are away.
He's on his own.

His mouth is a line
cold as the frost
which furs the fence
and the garden shed.
The earth is hard.
The world's in bed.

He stands as still
as bloodless stone,
unnoticed, he thinks,
by anyone.
In this, he is wrong.

On the roof-tops
starlings gather.
Sparrows feather the birch
like leaves.
They watch him get
a knife to cut
the black-in-white,
the dark, sweet bread.

Philpott aches
for the Christmas cake,
the slice he took
for someone's sake
who isn't here.

How can he eat?
He has no heart—
just cake—to break
at the bleak front door.

Clumsy and numb,
he scatters outside
currant and crumb

and the small birds come.

Leaving

'I will leave you, George. I will go.'
Easy to say
but her voice wavered.

'I'll go. One day you'll wake
and I will be flown.'
She said it too often.

The small birds in the garden
flew in and away.
She delayed.

Speedwell shimmered
in the blue lawn.
Her heart was long gone.

She went shopping
and found she hadn't returned.
It was done.

If she'd only known
as she watched, watched the small birds go,
that it would never be over,

over, over,
leaving in the spring,
in the winter leaving.

Cleaning

She cleans his upstairs bathroom
cleaner than any living soul.

She scrubs the bath with a nylon brush,
steams the tiles with her steam machine,
sprays with anti-bacterial spray,
polishes with a spotless cloth

and sometimes, as she cleans, she sings
in a high clear voice that no-one hears
but the bathroom and its silent walls
and the mirror and the laundered towels
and the patient, gleaming toilet bowl.

If this hadn't been her special gift,
perhaps that day as she stood in the hall
unhooking her coat from the pegs to leave

he wouldn't have noticed the gentle blush
dusting the inside curve of her arm.
He wouldn't have thought: it is like the rush
of light in the beech hedge when each hard bud,
surprised into softness, unfolds.

On Holiday at Auchterawe

I

Mr Philpott, sitting naked in the conservatory,
examines the clouds descending on Ben Tee
in a distant squall. The sun sips at his skin
urging an instant pinkness. Mrs Philpott
(she is his second wife; he calls her 'dear')
bears in their morning beverage on a tray.
She's wearing a fresh apron, embroidered with
roses. She sets the tray down and invites him
to put on the Welsh Male Choirs—put them on *loud.*
Her wish is his command. Removing his glasses, he
flicks a switch which swells men's voices into
exultation, flooding the world with a surge
of joy. Outside the rain comes down in sheets.
Inside, the milk discreetly cools the tea.

II

On holiday without her children, Mrs Philpott
washes the towels and waits for them to dry.
Mr Philpott has gone up the burn with his rod
and his waders. What are they doing now,
her distant, grown-up babies? Taller than her
and wiser, they have told her there's no use
regretting the past—the prams, the pushchairs.
Things, they say, move on, as people must, and she

should settle down, be positive, face it.
Each week, therefore, she lets herself unfold
a little curve of fat. Voluptuous,
as Mr Philpott calls it. 'Do you think,' he says,
'we're in love?' 'I want only you,' she replies.
Truth approaches. She doesn't embrace it.

III

In the conservatory, Philpott waits in the dark
with only the moon for company. They have had a row,
he and she, a marital discordancy, jangling of nerves.

Outside, the hills' grey curves and silvered thighs
swell into softness, rain slipping slow and steady
as heartbeats. Inside, the silence swells and forms

a statement: absence of love, absence of love.
He absorbs the repetition, hearing her move
in the distant house, somewhere near but far. Packing

perhaps. Folding neat underwear, sheathing cool silk
in a calm, green suitcase which travels well. He reaches
at last for the Welsh voices. Choral remedies—

can they suffice? Hands trembling, he pauses, then bravely
selects the right track. Perhaps he may yet be saved.

IV

Philpott wakes in the blue bedroom. Beside him
she dozes, her soft white shoulders curving
into dreams. Between the open curtains, sun
spills from the conservatory, where saving
graces still are dancing. Sleepless, Philpott
counts his losses one by one. He has lost
his sons, his thin first wife, his confidence—

all of them gone. He turns to his cowrie shell
of safety, slipping one arm beneath her neck,
the other round her waist in the way she likes
(or he thinks she likes). Very soon, he reflects,
there'll be toast and marmalade, the home-made, sweet-
bitter conserve of love. 'Ah George,' she moans
in her sleep. '*George.*' It is not his name.

V

George is not his name. But George isn't here—thus
Philpott consoles himself. Sadly he flies off
to sleep, airy and feathered. Mrs Philpott

is dreaming of pigs, a whole herd of them, and she's riding
the chief boar, clinging to yellow tusks. Spines cut
her inner thighs, searing the skin. 'Stop!' she cries

but the ride goes harder, faster, until the beast
rears his huge head. It's George, her first husband,
he has got her now. 'Dear George,' she pleads—

'George, let me go.' *No, no by the hair on my*
chinny-chin-chin, he snaps, beard extended.
Almost too late, a white bird drops, enfolding her

in its wings. 'You are voluptuous,' it sings. 'Come.'
She embraces, sobbing, the man who is holding her.

Leaving the Holiday House

The windows are shut, the rug shaken,
the bath scrubbed, the sheets folded,
the dishes washed, the floors hoovered,
the fridge polished (inside and out),
the kitchen surfaces sprayed and buffed,
the ornaments dusted, the dusters washed.

Their pictures are still in the camera,
clothes and socks in the suitcases,
memories packed inside their heads.
The car is waiting, its engine running.

All traces of them have been expunged.
They are unimportant, have killed no-one.

— || —

Seeing

Philpott's mother is ninety-one
with eyes as bright as silver sixpences.
In his right hand, her son could lift her

but doesn't lift her. Once she saw
in the new, pink shriek of his mouth
terror unmended by rocking a cradle.

The burden of seeing has bent her spine
and closed her ears.

When tea-leaves whisper from bone china
old Mrs Philpott sips a deep sweetness.

Curtains

Once she slept in a pink room
with another husband and closed drapes
but now the walls are trickled with green,
rising in stripes to a corniced ceiling—
and Philpott prefers the curtains open.

In solemn ritual every night
he puts on his carefully ironed pyjamas,
steps to the window, opens the curtains,
peers at the night, sighs once or twice,
climbs into bed and falls asleep.

Often she finds it hard to follow.
The white moon washes her laundered pillows.
His sleeping skin smells of new grass.
Sometimes she is possessed by lust,
sometimes by overwhelming loss. Outside

the luminous sky looks in. The stars are remote
and see too much. The wind insists
on making a fuss, and no muffling curtains
keep it out. Moonlight selects
the polished dresser, the silver hairbrush,

the photographs: Philpott's two sons, smiling
and thin; her unforgiving and angry daughters,
one on a skateboard; the children's dog.
Too dark to see, but all of them there
waiting, like her, for the Resurrection

when graves will open and all of the world
will find itself in the promised frame:
man and first wife forever unsundered,
flesh of that flesh, bone of that bone
joined in the terrible sight of God

in the pink room with the pink curtains
which clamp for ever around her heart
like the shut shell of a dead oyster.
'Oyster?' says Philpott, his shrimping net
trawling the rocks and pools of dreams.

'Give me fresh sole, I never eat oysters.'
'Hush,' she soothes, 'hush my darling—'
curving her warmth against his shoulder,
cradling his anxious meadow of skin,
facing the wide, uncurtained window.

Preserves

The sweetness of June, a summons conveyed
from strawberry fields, calls her to pick.
She drives to the farm, the car arrayed

with Tupperware tubs. Always she takes
only the small fruits, sips first and last,
careful to check the magic she makes

is subtle and true. At home, the jars
are washed and waiting, parched for the swell
of slick, thick lava reddened in glass.

In July it's raspberries that compel
the ritual feast. Nothing can stop
the droop of canes, the crimson bells

burdened with seeds and desperate to drop
in her open palm. Slowly she lets
the red juice seep. In jam, the sleep

of summer simmers, part of the heart
of the jam maker. She fires her pan
into melody and the music sets

rasps of ruby, sharp refrain
in a mildly labelled, covered pot.
The gentle house is calm again.

August. Brambles. Bold brash glut.
Black-mailed jelly. Bastard strain,
blood of the emperors, purple suit

potent as damson. This is no lean
harvest lament, no call to the weak
or lily-livered. The wild demesne

of darkness beckons. Soon she will take
a stick to the hedge-rows, bustle and shove
and conquer thickets, no less for the sake

of bramble jelly than slow-trickled love
through muslined October and late November
and then to the bleaker days, the grave

memories buried in deep December
and long January, locked and still,
when each year she almost forgets to remember

the oranges—saviours from Seville,
the unlikely, lumpy friends. She ought to
make ready sooner. She runs to fill

her jam pan with oranges, covers with water
and heats. Listen. The whole house is made
safe with the song, the smell of laughter.

Flood of light in a forest glade.
Sweet-bitter sunset. Marmalade.

Stopping

Philpott is very tired. He would like to stop.

He would like time. He would like time to be careful and slow
like the man down the road who trims the lawn
                          with his kitchen scissors.

He would like to watch the sun on the carpet,
watch it travel from the wall to the chair by the door.

He would like to listen to the noises of the house,
to hear the hair on his own arms stir.

Perhaps it's a sign. Ill people have to stop.
They stop and listen to the call of pain.

Perhaps illness is coming and he'd better move
quickly before it's too late, move quickly

before stopping happens. He isn't in pain
but this wanting to stop—it may be a sign.

Already he has keys in his hand, his leather briefcase
and his brisk face on. He has wasted an hour

and there's work to be done.

Life Insurance

The insurance man calls.
He mentions a matter of 'peace of mind'.
Mrs Philpott, who rarely gets angry,
is tempted to give him a piece of *her* mind.

All the money in all the pots and all the pantries of the world
doesn't buy peace. Not one piece of peace.
It's one thing worrying about a fridge.
You can fix a fridge, you can get a new one.
No earthly policy known to man
can compensate for a living person.

Of course, it may not come to that.
Mr Philpott writes him a cheque.
The man relaxes, picks up his hat.

Mrs Philpott goes to take
a corn-fed chicken out of the freezer.
Later her husband sees her
in the kitchen, at the window
watching the trees, the way the wind blows,
the way the leaves fall fast and and furious.

He stands very near her,
sees what she sees.
It is safer, closer.

Reckoning

It's never enough.
Philpott gets out the books and sighs.
All the time it is there, the burden of it,
thinking only, only of money.
Money on Monday and Tuesday and Wednesday,
money on Sunday
and the money files staring, cash and ledger,
share and stock, bond and yield,
red chips and blue.

His chair at the dining-room table is strong.
The parquet floor shines.
The table-top gleams with beeswax polish.
Sun interferes through the patio windows
with motes of dust. But the song in his head says
money, money and *never enough.*

In the garden the green-gold leaves of nasturtiums
open their faces like coins to the sky
and one flower opens, blood-red.

Philpott's dead wife had life insurance.
She left much money in place of herself.
It's never enough.

Offshore funds, equities,
gilts and derivatives,
futures and pasts.
There's a terrible cost, a terrible cost.

He scribbles a note, a crucial fact,
checks Friday's *Financial Times.*

His second wife puts a pheasant to roast
with thyme and chervil and rosemary,
then picks up her sewing—a tapestry

depicting a line of desert camels
making their way to an Arab tent.
She smiles at the thought of tent stitch for tents,
smiles and selects a mercerised strand.

Philpott feels something akin to despair
but drier and quieter.
He wants to stop counting.
He wants to enfold his lovely wife
and listen to life whispering in her thighs
and give up everything, save only this.

Mrs Philpott threads a camel
through the eye of her needle.

Money & Jam

Jam

It must be made and preserved
in pots with labels
and dates of making.
Sweet and sweeter, forsaking
all others, the last to be
and itself complete.
Who shall make it
if not she?

Money

It must be made
and then saved
with care and consent.
It must not be spent.
It has to be craved
and saved by degree
for the total amount,
for the final account.
Who shall save it
if not he?

Cake

Bake a cake for a visitor.
The baker is wearing a rose-bud apron.
Her hair and hands are dusted with flour.

Eggs are waiting beside the cooker.
The butter and sugar are beaten to foam.
The wooden spoon is charged with power.

This is a cake descended of cakes
born in small ovens for generations,
a cake of fragrance and careful making.

A hint of almond is for forgiveness;
the soft lemon curd is for contrition;
vanilla summons the shade of sweetness.

The crumb of the cake will be pale and warm.
The scent of the cake will be clear as dawn,
the shape of the cake a golden sun.

It will rise, like heaven, and then be gone.

— III —

Daughters

Both her daughters are angry with her.
Floor-boards creak, the chimney shivers.
Nobody now can stop or save her.

Time rages. She grows much smaller.
Fiercely she assails her mother
scared and stooping in the doorway.

Either she herself or other—
daughter-mother, mother-daughter—
rips the curtains from the window,

tears them to appease the daughters
who, in terror, seize and eat her
shrinking, lost to why or whether

both of them are mother-daughter,
each of them is daughter-mother.

Mrs Philpott's Dream

Rockabye baby on a tree top
when the wind blows the cradle will rock
when the wind blows   the baby wakes up

and Mrs Philpott thinks she wakes too
and runs (wind of the western seas) to the top
of the house where the baby is crying

where, where can the baby be?   lying
under the window in a moses basket
its little face framed in a lacy bonnet

and it isn't crying   it is very very quiet
she hasn't fed the baby for a long time
she can't remember when she last fed the baby

she lifts the baby up in her arms
bye baby bye baby bunting   daddy gone
quick into her arms where the baby belongs

and the baby smiles   it smiles   *look!*
but the baby must be hungry
she must find milk for the baby   quick

quick run to the kitchen   milk in the cupboard
quick   but what if the milk
is the wrong kind of milk   what if

the baby is under seven months old
it needs to be special milk gold top   and
when the bough breaks the baby will

quick put the gold-top baby down   mix
it and prick it and mark it with B
and put it on the table for baby   and

the baby has shrunk   there it is in the cradle
and it's tiny   it's half the size   when
when did she last feed the baby?   the baby

is shrinking   it's a quarter of the size
an eighth   she can hold the baby
in the palm of her hand   it will fall and

quick   catch the baby   it has gone
into a white comma   zipped back
inside her body   and she

really wakes up   and listens for the baby
but there is no baby

A Hesitation over Socks

Philpott has never hesitated over socks
until today. His hose lie ironed
in a special drawer, soles aired
in wool-rich patience, two by two
queued to be worn. On rising, he always
surveys the ranks, sweeping his gaze
across grey and blue, worsted and plain,
awaiting the surge, the groin tingle,
the firm herald saluting his choice.

But today droops, limp and uncertain.
No cockcrow of confidence, rush of the blood.
He stares at the mirror, seeing the briskness
drain from his face. Could he be ill?
A shuddered chill of winter encroaches
as (safe in her kitchen) his wife announces
irrelevant breakfast. He slumps on the bed,

collapsed to a sigh—and almost misses
the electrically obvious Royal Ramblers,
rich green footwear with feature toes,
a left foot and right, carefully hung
over the Dimplex in twinned content.
His manhood lifts and his heart with it.
Mrs Philpott has done it. She's laid them ready.
He pulls on his socks and his shoes and he walks
swiftly, smartly down every stair
to her unexpected self and kisses her.

Light

His father died at sixty-one
and so he will die at sixty-one
He fetches a tumbler.
Three years to go.

Soothed by Glen Livet
glittered on ice
he sits, he watches
the endless news:

floods and fires,
glaciers melting,
olympic games,
winners and losers.

His wife looks up
from her absent sewing.
Something about his face
is changing—

the lines round his eyes
are luminous.
A silver burnish
blesses his lips.

He is so still
that a kind of halo
spreading like grace
from inside his person

floods the room
and her hands with light.
She hardly knows
what to make of it.

Bird-watcher

Philpott, safe in his hide, records all that he sees
in the Insh Marshes, wetland of wader and gull.
He notes down the purple thyme, the visiting bees
and one buzzard, which circles precisely and falls
down a seam of invisible air to a blur of grass.

Such an ache for the sky inhabits the portly watcher
peering, binoculared, at untrodden grounds.
He yearns for the spotted crake, for the dowitcher,
and would, if he could, ascend. But his freckled hands
are not wings, merely tools of an aging, forgetful creature

who ought to go home. There's the fire to be laid,
wife to cajole. He is late. The newspaper nudges
its need to be read. There are meals to be paid for or made,
showers to fix. Meanwhile, the various sedges,
all twenty-six, have ripened and planted sharp seeds

in his brain. At bedtime he fidgets, fusses and sighs,
thinking of sex and bills and owls, until
sleep takes him, dropping from artexed skies
to glean his hot body. His spotted pyjamas cool,
he loosens his grip on the quilted earth and flies

out through the window and up to a flood of stars.
He's done this before. With practised restraint, he lets
the currents of swirling night bear him slow and far
over the marshes where great pools of silence, velvet
and deep, await. He circles, skims birch-tops, plummets—

wakes up and descends to breakfast, smears lemon curd
on his toast, informs Mrs P. how osprey defend
the nest. She remarks (as so often before) how absurd
it is for a man of his age to spend every weekend
in a hut—like a hermit—and all just to look at some bird.

Mutely he fetches in logs, the fresh split timber
of last year's tree. He winnows soft ash to a pile,
puts kindling in criss-crossed sticks over sleeping embers,
then stalls, puzzled, somewhere halfway to a smile
as a spark flies. He can't quite—perhaps—remembers.

Children

Each is, at times, a child to the other:
each a mother, each a father
and each, when charged with an adult fear,
a huddled, young conspirator.

Far from hollow hospitals,
the Philpotts play Monopoly;
the little houses ache to hold
hotels of eternity.

The banker says that death's not real.
The mortgage has been paid in full.

Night

At night Mrs Philpott lets down her hair,
she takes out the clasps and her hair tumbles.
Once copper, now silver, her hair ripples
and flickers her neck and her white shoulders.
She sits on the chair, sits and remembers
and brushes her hair, and brushes and brushes.

Her husband is watching. Not looking, but watching
the light on her hair, on her hair and her arm
and the strong strokes of her hand brushing,
the calm edge of her elbow turning,
the shadows that dimple her arm moving,
the clean sheen of her skin glistening

and the light on her hair in the room rushing
is like the spirit of water spilling
and falling over her living shoulders
and filling the air and the deep mirror
and bringing this man to an inner trembling
which nothing before in his life has ushered.

Perhaps he will lift the light up in armfuls
and give it again to the woman waiting
with love in her eyes and barely breathing
and hair, once copper, now silver glittering,
paused at last, and wondering—fearing—
hand on the hair brush poised and shivering.

Love

He has tipped, he has spilled
his soul into her
and she carries it still
like starlight on water.

— IV —

Regret

She shouldn't have left her husband and children.
She should have tried harder, ought to have known

that once you've done what you shouldn't have done
you can't just turn to another person

looking for love and absolution—
you have to make wilderness into your home.

She shouldn't have stumbled from being alone
into kind hands. She had done wrong.

Headache

Mrs Philpott pads painfully down the stairs,
one step at a time. Her fingers feel for the banister
in the rich dark. The carpet whispers

slow, slow. The house is peopled by creaks.
A line of grey is the kitchen door.
Slatted blinds slice up the night.

She strokes the big fridge. It purrs and hums.
Her headache mutters *come on, come on*.
She pulls the door open. Loud light drums.

Milk. She needs milk to help her sleep
and magical pills for her jagged brain.
She gulps the liquid straight from the jug.

The fridge whines. She makes no response.
She has to get back, somehow, to bed
over the daggers of *up* and *stairs*.

In their king-sized cot by the open window
Philpott is snoring under the stars.
She lifts the duvet and slips inside.

Her body is milk and dazzled moon.
She floods the pool of her sleeping self.
He dreams she's discovered a way to drown.

Getting there

Mrs Philpott, who doesn't like driving, drives.
Philpott, who does like driving, doesn't.

He's feeling dizzy. Blames the wine
or whisky or water. Of course, he's fine

but sighs whenever she goes too fast
and sighs again when she goes too slow

or much too close to the Saab in front
or hits the brakes for a bird. She knows

that the sigh of sighs as the car arrives
is relief. She has got him there, at last.

The Vengeance of Inanimate Objects

On Philpott's holidays it rains for spite.
His brother doesn't phone although he said he might.
The waist of his trousers is too tight.

Something in his spectacles loosens, falls
and a lens pops out. The blurred world reels.
He crawls on his knees, searching by feel

till his foot kicks the table and upsets a cup
of luke-warm coffee. Drip. *Drip.*
He's utterly soaked. Can't get himself up,

locate the lens (the imbecile chairs
are all in the way) or the tiny screw. He glares
and curses. Meanwhile a voice is singing upstairs

about rage (is it 'rage'?) that imprisons the heart.
Philpott stops breathing. Stops and listens.
In the green carpet, his need glistens.

Birthday

Sixty-one. And so he counts
the birthday cards he hasn't got.
Nothing from either son again
or from his brother in Condicote.
No card from his mother (who never forgets),
only one envelope, square on the mat
and it's from his wife. *With love from Val*
and five kisses. How he hates birthdays!
Fuss, fuss. Inordinate fuss.
He scrutinises the terrible card
which features an unconvincing trout
and fishing rod. Ridiculous
to have to look pleased, enduring this.
He heaves a sigh. His tea is poured
and breakfast looms. There on the dresser
a parcel lurks, wrapped with a bow.
Whatever next? He shakes his head
(fuss, fuss) as the toast comes in.
Then it gets worse. She disappears
and brings in a cake, the candles lit—
one per decade and one for luck.
He tries to smile but it doesn't work.
A traitor tear splashes his plate.
He blows his nose and the cups shake
and the tea-spoon rattles inside the saucer.
Fuss, *fuss*. He huffs out the flames
and cuts the first slice, wishing intensely
he didn't hate fuss and fancy food.
Sixty-one. He chances a bite.
The cake—tastes—remarkably good.

Choices

Shopping fills him
with desperation.
Here be demons
with gnashing trolleys
all of them rushing

with screaming infants
from apples to ketchup,
bleach to fajitas.
The tannoy roars.
They only run faster.

She leaves him to cower
alone by the PET FOOD.
From here, he can see
a queue at one checkout
incredibly short.

He hurries along
to FROZEN GOODS
where she's lost in thought
between chips and peas.

'Look there's our chance!
If we go now—'
With fevered brow
he points to the checkout.

She doesn't react.
The predicament's clear.
Bird's Eye or Savers?
She just doesn't know.

Candles

Each night brings silent argument.
Their strife is just impediment.

She rattles a box of safety matches.
Sulphur—the *smell!* Appalled, he watches

her strike and the living flames expand.
He switches on the extractor fan.

She carries two tall, illumined wands
to the table. Time, he understands,

to set down his pride, freshly-seared.
By candle-light, they swallow it.

Anger

Sometimes his rage lives in his shoes.
It tangles in his laces
and he wrestles like a lover

until it transforms.
He tries to hold on—
but the battle is long.

First his dead wife,
whose fingers are strong,
enters the ring

and he struggles with her, struggles
till she turns back to anger
and leaves a new danger.

It's his tall son, first-born,
a wiry fighter,
who takes on his father

and there's no winning
the tugging and straining,
no owning, disowning

but only the noose, the noose of life
that pulls too tight
and won't be appeased

and the knots are fast,
their fury rolls
from tongue to throat

from eyelet to sole.

Visitor

Illness, leaning on a stick, stands by the fire.
No-one invited him.
None of the ceremonies are secure.

His eyes are intimate, familiar.
All his old friends are doctors.
Slowly he raises one blue finger.

There were only two people living here.
Now there are three.
Illness is related to marriage by despair.

He means to unlock his black mouth and speak.
On the instant, Philpott is awake.
He is awake and shivering in his bed which is like the sea,

a turmoil of waves and no shore
and his wife in the sheets, her glass eyes open,
sees too much in the dark, too far

and between them a thin, cold presence lies—
the silent body of the visitor.

Wedlock

Still the sweet illogical knot
tightens with every year.
He loves her. Why? Because she loves him.
And she? Because he loves her.

How it begins or how it will end
they will not (how can they?) say.
Sufficient unto the waking hour
the livery of the day.

— V —

Flaws

The day has had numerous imperfections.
The gravy, for example. She hasn't made it like he *likes*
although he doesn't say. Only a sigh tells her.
Like the sigh when his walking boots are not to hand
and the instant when he takes a sip of tea
to find they both have sugared it.

      But equally
the sunlight on the fence
is warm. He finds his hand in hers
and the thought occurs
that he may even have been—
one day when he looks back on it—
happy.

Christmas

Philpott has no time for cards,
disliking polar bears and holly wreaths
and mice with mistletoe.
In Advent he commences seething.

Mrs Philpott is resigned.
Making no open challenge, she
wraps packets for the grandchildren
and takes them to the Post Office

wondering why the western world
makes disproportionate seasonal fuss,
equalled alone in this hemisphere
by her husband's disgust.

The heralds of imminent torture
are carol singers on Christmas Eve.
Philpott stomps noisily up to bed
with a copy of *Bird Watching Magazine.*

On the fateful morn, inevitably
he stumbles awake at six o'clock,
shuffles on pants and socks. *Socks?*
Inside the toe of every one—

the whole infested drawer of them—
someone has slipped a chocolate coin.
His slumbering wife gives nothing away,
dreaming of snow and elves and Santa.

Scratching his head perplexedly
Nicholas Philpott goes for a shave,
lathering clouds of billowed foam
onto a barely stubbled face

which stares back at him in some surprise.
His eyes! They're sparkling, or nearly.
And how white, how *very* white his 'beard'.
He could almost be taken for ... merry.

Absence

Not always loving the one he loves
he meditates on the absence of love
and makes a consequent mountain of

a stone in the street which isn't flat.
A disgrace. It's a matter of what
They know They should do but do not.

Next day he hardly looks at her at all.
He cares neither for the call
of the curlew, nor the long shadow in the hall.

Truth. Where can it be and why?
'Do you love me?' she says. 'Really?'
He can't manage a reply.

He's a piled-up cairn on a mountain
and his silent heart is a stone.
Without meaning to go, he has gone.

Peace

Philpott comes home, his briefcase stacked.
He kisses her wearily, slumps in his chair.
'We must watch the war.'

Black once more, the news from Iraq:
a broken child wrapped in a cloth.
Mrs Philpott puts both hands to her mouth

and vanishes into the kitchen where
she soon disinfects the spotless hob.
Women, she thinks, wouldn't make wars—

women would NOT as she sprays as she wipes
as she scrubs would NOT as she buffs as she rubs
would NOT would NOT as she takes on the dirt

that doesn't exist, her teeth clenched tight
wouldn't crush wouldn't kill as she bristles and scours—
wouldn't make WARS

and in the sitting-room Philpott sighs
and his sigh rises up for comfort and flies
to the kitchen where she washes it too—

a dip in the sink, a drop of bleach.
She'll teach this sigh, this air-borne breath
to go in peace. She will not have death.

69

Reflection

Their entire lives are reflected in the side of the kettle.
Every detail. His glasses. His book. The metal
of mettles. The lamp. The flicker of flames.
The TV. The board games. Even the blur
where he sits in a cloud
and waits
for her.

Relations

Sex may still occur
though it's unpredictable.

She (the non-initiator)
finds him willing
but not able

or (it would appear)
able but uneager.

For her
sex is love
and loving.

For him
it is high risk—
if thrilling.

Banished

It's a bad day. They leave the garden
sheltered by only a giant umbrella.
They wear their stout boots and avoid puddles.

They walk and walk, and start to climb
to the stopping place where they always look
over the trees to the gleaming loch

but all they can see is mist rising
and the red and white stripes of the bright umbrella.
He lifts it high with portly bravado.

She shivers close and clings to his arm.
They wait on the hill, cold and alone.
They have lost the world

and the rain comes down.

Why

Why (he is always thinking)
does she have to make dinner so soon?

Why does she move the curtains
and block the light of the moon?

Why does she sneeze again and again
at the faintest suspicion of fluff?

Why does she clean the shower three times
when *once* is more than enough?

Need

She doesn't yearn for him
as he yearns for her

but in the night
when the stars grow dim

and he turns to her,
she turns to him.

— VI—

Ironing

She will be ironing.
He will be watching The News.

Out of the corner of his eye, he will see
her right arm sweeping this way and that,
her head inclined.

She will be pressing the tablecloth
that her mother embroidered.
She will be lifting and smoothing and folding.
The cloth will be heavy and hot.

She will be thinking and thinking about
the nature of love (her mother had little)
and the nature of faith (her mother had much)
and the trickiness of material corners—
to sew in the first place, to iron in the second.

He will be noticing the way she is paying
minute attention to the matter in hand.
He will be taking (without even knowing)
a picture to keep somewhere in his mind.

She will be wondering if it's worth more
when a thing is hard, and whether she has
the skill for the task. She will be tested
and sorely tried by the bruising sole
of her turbo-steam iron.

He will keep something inside himself
that he'll never, not now, not ever forget.

But this hasn't happened
yet.

Garden

balmy air   wicker chair
     floral dress   floppy hat
   August day   far away
    lacy wings   zooming low
      breathing in   breathing out
floral print   floppy brim
       bumble bee   on her knee

    buzzing soft   being bee
     busy stir   dozy blur
  being him

       being her

Risk

Should anyone call,
it increases the chance
of intense agitation
to which he is prone.

If they go for a stroll,
it enhances the chance
of not being there,
should anyone phone.

Should anxiety rise,
she will need to stay calm.
This is a matter
of which they don't speak

but the risk being high
she chances her arm.
'I'll get the umbrella.
We'll go for a walk.'

Dinner

Late in the evening sun
food is plain and good.

They're hungry, both of them.
They make short work of it.

The dining table shines.
Never a time more sweet

only to sit like this,
only to sit and eat.

Anniversary

Who can find a virtuous woman? For her price is above rubies.

He takes the train.
He goes to a place
that sells the best.
He invests
in a necklace
of South Sea pearls
(because she loves pearls).

He takes out
his cheque book.
His face is grave.
He commits by number
to days without number
and signs his name.

Rain

Philpott always expects the worst
though the worst hasn't happened yet.
He presumes it will rain on holiday,
and to tell the truth it usually does
but rarely as much as he expects.

Their recently-serviced car, he says,
may not make it as far as Perth—
there's something not right, or about to be.
It will never get them to Auchterawe.
But it does. And the burn is full of rain

and the clouds are low and grey, and so
it's good that he packed the big umbrella,
the waterproofs and the walking boots.
It's good that he always plans for the rain
though he hopes against hope against hope
against hope

for the best.

Fault

He's ill. It's not his fault
but she blames him anyway.
He won't exercise. Or eat.

He drinks. And blames himself.

Not her fault that he wears his blame
as a guerdon.
How hard it is to get him up!

By rule of her careful thumb

she measures the way the balance shifts,
the weight of his wealth
on each of his shoulders. She is the prop.

She stoops, and breathes
and lifts.

The Hill

His heart is okay (it has been checked)
but not far from the top his pace is checked

and he stops. 'Enough. Let's go back.'
Mrs Philpott doesn't want to go back.

If they get to the summit, they'll see the view.
He doesn't give tuppence about the view.

'It's not far,' she says.
                              'Too far,' he says.
She doesn't care a bit what he says,

she wants to get to the top of the hill. 'Come on,'
she says. 'Best foot forward.'
                              'You go on,'

he says. 'I'll wait here.' So she walks on her own
and quickly sets up a pace of her own

not pausing and not once looking back
until for some reason she stops and looks back

and he's quite out of sight, could be anywhere
and a sort of fear catches her where

head and heart meet. This stupid emotion is love
and because of that, because of her love,

if *he* won't get to the top of the hill,
then *she* won't get to the top of the hill

either. Anyway, a few drops of rain
fall on her hair and she knows he hates rain.

He might even have turned
and gone home without her. She turns

and half-runs down the path. He's waiting for her,
sitting on his coat and waiting for her.

'About time,' he says. 'Where have you been?'
She says, 'Where do you *think* I've been?'

He doesn't ask about the view from the top.
She doesn't tell him she didn't get to the top.

She might think, 'This is the story of my life,'
but although this is the story of her life

that is not what she thinks.
She thinks something else.

— VII —

What He Can't Stand

Queues in the bank, weeping women, smart alecs,
wide boys, cigarette smoke, barbecue reek,
mobile phones, slow drivers *Come on!*

Boy racers, sleeping policemen
drivers who hesitate at roundabouts
drivers who don't indicate
slow drivers who can't decide
crawlers in the fast lane *Come on, come on!*

Taps dripping, hinges creaking, dogs barking,
cats scrapping, cars crawling, fan-belts squealing

Christmas and birthdays
Zadok the Priest
dirty glasses
cheap whisky

Tea with no sugar, tomato ketchup, pasta in any shape
or form, Inland Revenue, smartarses, fatuous fools
Come on, come on, come on!

All of it, all of it, all of it is
driving him mad

The Spaces in the House

Two people are living
in a house with sundry spaces
in which
each person
is alone.

The upstairs bathroom
and the downstairs toilet
are solitary places.

The sewing room is
a fine and lonely spot
from which
a man can look
right down the street

to where
a woman in the distance
is approaching
with her shopping
and her hat.

No matter if the shopper
comes in with silly offers
of coffee
and/or
cake.

The wingback chair
beside the fire
is all a body
could desire
(though later
he may partake).

Tense

'Why are you looking tense?' she says.
Mistake.

His tenseness is designed
to be invisible. It's the stretch
of years, the sheer extent

of things undone
and things unsaid,
the toll of self
by self despised
and day by day
re-lived.

Tense? *tense?*

He isn't tense!
He's in despair.
Not everything
can be relieved.

She draws the curtains.
She lights the lamps.
It isn't everything
but it's something.

She offers three things:
a bowl of soup,
a plate of bread,
a seat by the fire as night draws in.

Earworm

There was a banker had a wife
And Hilda was her name O.

H I L D A
H I L D A
H I L D A
And Hilda was her name O.

There was a banker's wife got ill
And Hilda was her name O.

clap   I L D A
clap   I L D A
clap   I L D A
And Hilda was her name O.

There was a banker's wife who died
And Hilda was her name O.

clap clap   Hilda died
clap clap   Hilda died
clap clap   Hilda died
And Hilda was her name O.

Clap-clap-clapping. Sing-sing-singing.
What's going on?
He *never* sings!

His eyes are watering, the stupid things.

Mrs Philpott is crying.

The Mood

He was in a terrible mood.
It was so terrible that the sun went out and the air was thin.
It was so terrible she was sucked in.

Inside the mood the bathroom had no soap.
The fire wouldn't light. The heating bill was huge.
The washing machine broke.
There was no hope.

They went to the shops and it rained.
'This is the way it will be from now on.
You hating me, me hating you. Get me a gun!'

He was a gigantic thistle, purple and bristling.
She shrank to a harebell. They had no idea
the world was only a mood

until a boy walked past them. *Whistling.*

— VIII —

Back

'What have you done to the bed?' she says,
tucking the corners back into place,
smoothing the coverlet, tweaking the lace.

'It was the women,' he says, 'those women—
such a fuss and bother in bed.'

There are no women. *She* is the woman.
'Two days at my sister's,' (she shakes her head)
'and what do you DO to this poor bed?'

'Blame the women,' he says, and takes
her lavender suitcase and puts it away
under the stairs where the hoover lives.

She is back. He is glad. And the bed is glad
and a pot of coffee is almost ready.

Safe

'That miserable old skinflint,'
is what Mrs Philpott's youngest daughter says
about her mother's second husband.

There is some truth in this description.
Most of the time he is miserable.
He is old, too, compared to her daughter.
And flinty, yes.
As flinty as the Neolithic mines at the Den of Boddam
where he may once have seen a Montagu's Harrier.

The daughter thinks he has no heart.
'All he cares about since he retired,' she says,
'is stocks, shares, and the combination lock
of the dining-room safe.'

She's partly right (he is a worrier
and these things are matters of concern)
but not right about the heart

because he certainly possesses one.
Mrs Philpott has it for safe-keeping
(she proposed this and he willingly agreed).
She keeps it nice and clean in a place apart.
His heart is safe. Few hearts are safer
or more rarely seen.

The Change

The sun was bright but low in the sky.
Philpott was driving and light was flashing.
He could not, could NOT
see where he was going.

There was no air.
He slammed on the brakes
and his hands were shaking,
all of him shaking.

She took the wheel, while he sat tense—
tense and intense—
in the passenger seat.
He shouted, he bellowed.

The car behind was driving too CLOSE.
There were CRACKS in the road.
The sun was BLINDING.
The visor was USELESS.

Simmering tension turns into rage,
and rage into fear.
Low sunlight
preys on the mind.

But how on earth
has it come to this?
How has she seen
what nobody sees?

Understanding

It's happening a lot.
She'll turn and she'll find him
standing beside her,
lost in thought.

He may stand, for example,
not far from the window,
his face as blank
as a stopped clock.

Or when she's cooking,
without any warning
he's there in the doorway,
a standing stone.

He stands there
on standby. Why?
No word, no gesture,
no explanation.

If only she knew
(she finds herself thinking)
how to read his mind,
how to understand.

But what can it mean
for her ageing husband
to take up his station
like this, unmoving —

to stand, to stand
and continue to stand?

Pause

Some days Philpott
tries to pace
from room to room,
space to space,
in the usual way
but his feet slur.

He moves like a man
going down and down
in slow motion
to the treacly bottom
of thick ocean

an ocean with a kitchen
where Mrs P is washing up
raising a cup
to the light,
getting it clean,
getting it perfectly
polished and pure

though something
has caused her
to time-slip. In fact,
there's many a slip
betwixt cup and—

—it's paused her—
look—

right here
right
now

Dream

He's lost his car in his sleep. It was in the car park,
not on the second floor beside the concrete pillar
but on the third floor beside the concrete pillar.
In his head, he retraces his steps. He drove into town,
he parked the car beside the pillar on the third—
yes, the *third* floor.

He paces the car park. Could he have parked it
in the other car park where nobody goes?
He walks through the wall into a building,
a department store. He needs to get
to the car-park exit, but most of the doors
are bedroom doors or cleaning cupboards.

When he sees Mrs Philpott, what a relief!
He met her that morning. She must remember
from which direction he had been walking.
'The car can't be far,' she says. 'You were carrying
your overcoat and your leather briefcase.'

But where are they now?
Where on earth is his leather briefcase?
Where on earth is his Ford Mondeo?

Together they wander
right round the building in search of the door
that leads to the car park in which perhaps
he did park the car. There are spiral stairs
and a thin cleaner with a Russian accent
who mutters 'Five hundred and fifty-five.'

When Philpott wakes up, he says nothing of this.
He goes to check on his leather briefcase
carefully placed in its usual space.
Mrs Philpott gets up and goes straight to the window
to see if the car is parked in the drive.
Which it is. Thank heavens—it *is*.

Sausage Rolls at Hogmanay

Mr Philpott is wearing a small frown
which he denies. The matter?
Nothing. Danger flickers
in the furrows on his brow

so Mrs Philpott goes quickly
into the kitchen where
sausages are meek
and mild and the pastry

waits without favour or fear
to be turned and turned again.
Her rolling pin is as fair
as the moon at New Year

into which the fury of the old
is rolled.

— IX —

Communication

Philpott speaks the language of sighs
which is a language of pure emotion
made only of air

and the language of sighs is not his wife's language—
she doesn't speak it but learns to interpret
the tiniest nuance,

the smallest verb of the glossary
of the language of men whose deepest feeling
is too raw for words,

too naked for clothing, although her husband
(whose eloquence is never in doubt)
doesn't know what he says,

what his heart gives away, as his breath expresses
his sorrow, his fear, his rage, his loss
and even his love.

January

He heard her say, *It's snowing.*
(She really said, 'You're snoring'.)

He snored on through the falling snow,
flakes heaped on his sleeping brow

but because of the snow it was slow going
with a snore of white and drifts growing

though the fleece of the freeze seemed to be easing
his shoulders and back and hips and knees

in a quilted comfort far from the world
of dread and payment and pearls unpurled

and when she cried out, 'Nicholas! You're snoring!'
he heard her say *How thickly it's snowing!*

and sank even deeper, deeper than deep,
careless of snowing, careless of sheep,

careless of snore and financial concern,
zero investment in a return.

Repetitions

What can be worse
than saying the same thing twice?

Saying it three times? Or four?
Or more?

At the moment, it's twice.
She has said the same thing twice—the *same*—
and takes no notice

until he's irate. Consumed with fury.
You said that ALREADY!

She's startled.
Then laughs.

There are appropriate reactions.
Others are inappropriate.

He wants to hammer the wall with his fist
but that wouldn't do.

The wall is not to blame.
The wall is not.

Separation

i

Mrs Philpott goes to bed alone.
The clock in the hall ticks on.
Philpott turns to cut glass, then stone.

All the things we do to be loved,
all of them pointless.
The clock ticks on.

Nothing but moonlight dawns.
The distance from downstairs
to upstairs yawns.

Philpott sags and snoozes alone
in the wishing chair,
in the wishing air.

All the things we do to be loved—
in the night they slip far away.
It will never be day.

The clock ticks on
as well it may.

ii

She wakes first. He has not slept
in the chair all night.

At first light
he has crept

into the bed on the other side.
He will not (cannot) say it, but

everything about him is sorry—
only half of him is under the duvet

and his eyes aren't really shut.
She pulls the covers over them both and he falls

into a sleep as deep and sound
as a lost child who has wandered far out of sight

(while his mother calls and calls and calls)
and is finally found.

Accusation

'You came to bed,' she said,
'leaving all the lights blazing!'

A rare admonition,
though they weren't blazing.
There were simply *on*

like the human brain
when a response
of no-response

gives scant
illumination.

— X —

Polish

Truth to tell, Mrs P
is also prone to occasional gloom
which she dissolves by polishing

the glass-topped table,
the empty bath,
the square tiles on the kitchen floor.
They must be clean,
they shall be clean!

She summons the light from dark places
to make a response
in the gleaming mirror
to one fair question

and her answer shines.

Sheets

Quality products. All is not lost
with organic sheets, Egyptian cotton,
400 thread count, as white as white.

Then there's the frost.
It whitens the sheets like nothing else
and a top-notch iron sorts out the creases,
smoothing out hems and flattening folds.
White sheets for night.

A bed is no bed without such sheets
and hospital corners holding them tight,
pillows popped neatly into their cases.

And some people like a bolster too,
soft with eider-duck feathers, king-sized,
sheathed in a quality cotton slip.

The bed is bolstered and true, dear heart,
ready for billowing seas, your ship.

'The Joy of Sex'

Nicholas Philpott isn't skilled at sex
although he thinks he is.
His second wife knows about socks
and anxiety. She doesn't miss
the tattered copy of *The Joy of Sex*
once purchased by her husband's ex.

That doesn't mean it's easy.
There's sex, and there's intimacy.
There's intimacy, and there's sex.
Neither leads invariably to the next.

First wife

It's always there. Like air.
And sometimes, though nearly invisible,
it swirls like mist so it's hard to see
anything clear but fear.

It can make itself into shapes.
Soon (she isn't yet here)
it's going to be *her*.

There she is, beside the privet!
She limps to the window,
tipping her face and peering in.
She's achingly thin.

She reaches right through—
right through the glass—
and catches his throat.
His colour is grey
and his legs have frozen.

The second Mrs Philpott
comes into the room
and touches his face.
Hardly a flicker,
he's nearly gone.

She looks through his eyes,
sees what he sees
and why she was chosen.

She fetches a glass of pure water
and places it
in his good right hand.
What if it fails?

He lifts. He sips.
He sips. He lifts.
He looks at the window.
He closes his eyes.

He opens his eyes.
He looks at the window.
He takes a deep breath.
Exhales.

'Thank you, my love.'
Then: 'Some ice
would be nice.'

Revenant

Could have, should have,
should have, could have,
would have, didn't

and there she is again,
this time in a ridiculous hat
with a smile more like a smirk.

Would have, should have,
should have, would have,
might have, didn't

and that's why she's calling,
this time in her nightie
and a blink more like a wink.

Didn't, couldn't,
ought to have, wouldn't,
ought to have *said*

but she's saying it now,
with her pointing finger
and nail more like a knife.

Hallucination

He's thinking about the word 'hallucination'
and whether he's had one.
Is he seeing things?

'Ratiocination'. *There's* another word to conjure with.
He's not seeing clearly, but he's thinking clearly
about thinking and whether his own brain
is down the Swanee.

It happens to the best of us. We go, or bits of us
depart. The head, the heavy hip joints. The heart.
No-one's ever ready for this breakage, bit by bit,
this losing of grip.

You don't expect to watch your own disintegration.
It should happen without you knowing,
                            gone without going,
suddenly, with just a brief pain.

He has no pain
but he's seen things that aren't there. He has seen *her.*
Is it guilt? Has guilt brought her back?

'Did you see—' he starts to say to his wife
and stops because
she's nodding
and white as a sheet.

So they're both mad.
He cheers up.
He finds he can eat his toast
and swaps the word 'hallucination'
for 'ghost'.

Death Comes for the Philpotts

The first Mrs Philpott is dead.
The second will die too.
But not yet, not yet.

If he goes first,
as you might expect,
she will turn to her work.

She will have to inspect
the spick and the span,
the dust and the drain.

She will deep-clean
the bedroom, the kitchen,
the bathroom, the hearth.

She will play her part,
she will ply her art.

And when she is done
(she will never be done)
she may take his shade
in her arms and lie down.

If *she* goes first
(if life is unkind
and his worst fear comes true)

he will enter his mind
for old times' sake
by forcing the gates

of the old abyss
that drops him
in fathoms
(unfathomed
unguessed)
into the shadows
of old despair

and find her there
brushing and brushing
her hair

shining

silver

paused

— XI —

Sleet

'Things change, and not for the better,'
Philpott points out. They're building new houses
along the old road overlooking the loch,
felling some trees. The birds don't like it,
he doesn't like it. It starts to sleet,
thin slashes of snivelling grey
in April. *April!* The hills recede,
hidden in cloud.

Trapped in the house
he watches The News. Climate is changing,
trouble brewing. What's to be done?
Sighing, he lays the fire with sticks
and smokeless fuel and newspaper balls.

Mrs Philpott comes in, pink from her bath.
She looks through the window.
Perhaps, she thinks, she'll put on some soup.
Perhaps she'll bake.

But first she intends
to change the bed, to lift those old sheets
of fading white and put on the new ones
she bought in town: pale, soft green
with a pattern of daisies. Daisies, daisies,
a pattern of daisies.

Mrs Philpott and the Spiders

There is complicity between her
and the spiders of the house.

She dusts upstairs on Tuesday
downstairs Wednesday morning.
She takes a feather duster
to the ceilings and the corners
where webs first appear.
She brandishes a warning.

The spiders disappear
to invisible spaces.
while she removes their traces
from the visible places
and makes them clean and clear.

The spiders have
exactly one week
to recoup and repair
and kill a few flies.
The arrangement is fair.

Things Might Be Different

He might get up out of the chair.
He might stride over to the window
and say, 'How about some air?'

He might contemplate his paunch.
He might laugh at the healthy option
and say, 'How about some lunch?'

He might pick up the phone
and call one of his long-lost friends.
'Fancy a spot of fishing, John?'

Things might be different. Oh those poor things!
He made a sour face and the wind changed
and now he's rearranged.

If the wind would only change back,
with a little luck
he might get unstuck.

On Gloom and Proper Respect

He doesn't exactly blame her for it. No,
it's not her fault. She is the way she is—
incorrigibly optimistic. But
the strain of her unbridled cheerfulness

must tell. His gloom requires due diligence.
It's there to serve a need, and needs a slow
and proper processing. That's it—a proper processing. To this he must commit, and hence

his necessary isolation. No,
he is not depressed. He's just processing. Some 'thing' is passing through. It will go
eventually, but it must run its course.

The weight of doom would be a minor stress
if she would just dispense with cheerfulness.

Hurt

Now why must it be that he,
who loves her in very truth,
should speak to her disparagingly?

And she—understanding as best she may
the sorry weight of his needful heart—
why must she know this, but not in words

and therefore have to carry the hurt
(in a manner of speaking unexplained)
for them both?

Circle

They haven't been out in weeks
but he agrees to go. They walk
together but not touching
in the town park.

She returns on her own.
He's stuck out there alone.
Of course, it starts to rain.
There's sorrow that nobody sees.

It starts in the knees
and advances through the spine.
In the end you go home.
You're alive, so you live.

There's a lamp in the window
and she will forgive.
And there's tomorrow,
there's always tomorrow.

Turn

How has it got so bad?
From their funny-sad, almost glad
loving selves
to the sad-funny, half-mad
turning away.
How has it got so bad?

Luck

Mrs Philpott goes down on her knees in the lawn
looking for a four-leaved clover.

Philpott doesn't believe in luck. Or only the bad kind.
He gets out the mower.

'*Stand aside!*' he shouts as he cuts a swathe through the grass,
clover or no clover.

She gets up in haste, something green in her hand.
Some storms pass over.

— XII —

Pearls

I.

Philpott is slumped in his wing-backed chair
with the FT and Brexit. He flaps the newspaper
in despair. 'Where are these IDIOTS taking us now?'

She puts down her knitting. 'Into the woods?'
'If we must,' he responds, missing the point.
'Now where are my boots?'

So they go. They walk and they walk.
It's a long way on foot, but into the woods
they both disappear.

What happens next is somewhat unclear.
Something about an umbrella
and who should have brought it

gets out of hand. There's shouting,
there's pointing. Bad things are said.
He marches off and leaves her to stew

and there she is, alone in the woods
staring at something she's dropped
on the ground. She's shaking, and crying.

It really won't do. His rage is outrageous,
the look on his face the look of a stranger,
a *savage* stranger.

Forgiving wives can't always forgive.
They can't even—for God's sake—
forgive themselves

and now her beautiful pearls have broken.
They snapped like his temper and horrible words,
the pearls he bought her a decade ago,

all of a sudden, all by themselves,
a frivolous looseness about her neck,
a panic, a slither, a slip—a sign.

She pops the string silently into her bag.
A break at the clasp but the knotted beads
all safe but the one

that dropped at her feet in the mud
and shone.

He's raving, she thinks as she turns, he is *mad.*
He's like Uncle Jack (poor Uncle Jack)
who went for some treatment and didn't come back.

Having voiced the thought to herself at last,
she loses the plot and thinks he will lose
his way in the woods and die out there

in the dark on his own—that grown man raving
about an umbrella, that grown man who ought,
by now, to know better.

She abandons the lonely pearl to shine.
And wouldn't you know, it's starting to rain
and the sky is murky, he may not be safe

from the risk of himself
and he's prone to confusing the way through the trees
so although it's insane—frankly *insane*—

she gets out the necklace from inside her bag
and also her tiny emergency scissors
and snip, snip, snip
as she goes step by step

she drops the pearls faithfully
one
by
one

to light up the way
like miniature moons
in the sky of a person
who only looks down.

Madness. Pure madness.
Her priceless pearls—and all of them gone,
the very last one at the edge of the trees

from which she stumbles and hurries home
to put on a pot of vegetable soup.

2.

Philpott has a sensitive nose.
The scent of rain causes him pain.
He endures the slimy stink of the mud,
the smell of himself in the filthy wood
because he deserves it. The east wind changes
to south-south-west. He stomps along
in the wrong direction,
no sun, no moon, no bloody umbrella.
His brow is furrowed, his shoulders droop,
and he thinks he smells something like—
not *un*like—soup.

3.

Half-past six. He still isn't home.
She's thinking of phoning 999
when the door creaks open and in he steps,

stooped and weary, muddy and wet.
She holds out her arms (how could she not?)
and hugs him as close as his coat will allow.

I can't live without you, she hears him say,
although he says nothing, nothing at all.
'Nicholas, Nicholas—are you all right?'

He shakes his head. She holds him tight.
'I was lost in the woods. You fetched me back.
How did you do it?'

'You know quite well,' she says—relieved
that her plan with the pearls has actually worked,
that her precious beads are safe in his pocket.

He thinks she must know how he followed his nose,
how he followed the trail of the magical smell,
how it led him back home like a miracle.

His darkness slips off with his outdoor clothes
and he settles to eat. The smell unfurls
from the bread and the soup

and he swallows each mouthful
as slow as he can
and every drop warms
and every drop heals.

4.

'Now where,' she smiles,
as he empties the bowl,
'have you put them, my darling?

Where have you put
my beautiful pearls?'

Peril

He reaches for her. 'Are we all right?'

On a small boat in a dark sea
with no land, no light—
not even a star—
and the winter rising
sharp in the night

of course they are not all right

but she takes him in her arms
and she tells him that they are.